To My Dearest Lucy
much love Amy

My First
Buddhist Alphabet

My First
Buddhist Alphabet

Text by John and Natalie Bates
Illustrations by Peggy Mocine

TREASURE
TOWER
BOOKS

Published by Treasure Tower Books
The children's book division of the SGI-USA
606 Wilshire Blvd.
Santa Monica, CA 90401

© 2004 SGI-USA

ISBN 0-915678-79-9

Cover and interior design by
Linda Joe
SunDried Penguin Design

10 9 8 7 6 5 4 3 2 1

Library of Congress Cataloging-in-Publication Data

Bates, John.
My first Buddhist alphabet / text by John Bates, and Natalie Bates;
illustrations by Peggy Mocine.
     p. cm.
Summary: My First Buddhist alphabet is a children's book aimed for
three to seven year old children. It teaches the the children
some of the basic principles of Nichiren Buddhism in an easy to
understand format using the ABC alphabet and rhyming sounds.
ISBN 0-915678-79-9 (pbk. : alk. paper)
1. Nichiren, 1222-1282—Juvenile literature.
2. Soka Gakkai—Doctrines—Juvenile literature.
3. English language—Alphabet—Juvenile literature.
I. Bates, Natalie. II. Mocine, Peggy. III. Title.
BQ8349.N577B38 2004
294.3'928—dc22
2004015487

A is for Altar,
a wonderful place.
It's home for Gohonzon
with plants in a vase.
There's water and candles
and incense to smell.
It's where we can chant
until we feel swell!

B is for Buddha, a person who's sure
That life is wonderful, happy and pure.
It's not someone else, it's us at our best.
We want to be Buddhas, so we make it our quest.

C is for Chant, which we do every day.
Chanting Nam-myoho-renge-kyo is how we each pray.
A long time or short time, an hour or minute,
What matters most is that your heart's really in it!

D is for Daimoku,
the name of our chant.
When you're filled with daimoku,
there's no room for "can't."
Nam-myoho-renge-kyo works,
you can bet.
Whatever you chant for,
an answer you'll get.

I don't have a question. Just give me food and a warm lap.

Q: Will chanting help me make friends at my new school? A: Of course!

Q: Will chanting help me pass my spelling test? A: Yes, if you also study hard!

Q: May I sit in your lap while you chant? A: Yes, if you are good.

E is for Effect, the result of a cause.
When you sing a nice song,
  you get the applause.
But make a bad cause,
  like tripping a waiter,
And soup on your head
  is the effect you'll get later!

F is for Faith, which means being sure
That something is true, like two two's make four.
Faith at first means just give chanting a try,
Then you'll have actual proof to live by.

+

= 4

G is for Gohonzon,
  made of paper and ink.
It's so much more marvelous
  than you might think.
It works like a mirror
  to show us our power.
Nichiren Daishonin calls it
  our treasure tower.

H is for Hope,

a wish you believe in—
As bright as the stars
that you see in the evening.
How to make sure that
your hope never ends?
Think about others,
and share with your friends.

I means myself, and I have the power
To make my life bloom
  like a beautiful flower.
When I chant, there's no end
  to what I can create—
It takes just one
 "I" to make
  the world great!

J is for Justice, to know what is fair.
To stand up for justice means that we care
That all people everywhere have what they should:
Happiness, freedom and lives that are good.

K is for Karma.
   The causes we've made
Are part of our lives,
   and that's where they've stayed.
Some karma is good;
   but some gives us trouble.
When our karma is changed,
   we feel light as a bubble!

L is for Lotus,
   a flower that grows
Deep in the muddy swamp,
   which clearly shows
That people who practice
   and chant a whole lot
Find beauty and joy
   in the ugliest spot.

M is for Myoho, which we chant every day.
It means "Mystic Law"—it's to open the way.
Our faith turns the key that unlocks the door
And reveals all the wonders the world has in store.

N is for Nature, the world we inhabit—
From the tallest of trees to the littlest rabbit.
Bright stars and oceans, the rain and the sun—
The universe, nature and we are all one.

O is for Ourselves and it's also for Others—
All of us here, we are sisters and brothers.
They're part of our practice and you know it's true:
I'm chanting for me, and I'm chanting for you.

P is for Practice, which we do every day.
Gongyo and daimoku are the way that we pray.
We study and read, and we tell people, too,
About this great practice, and what it can do.

Q is for Questions.
   I'm sure you will find,
When looking for answers
   with your seeking mind,
Your wisdom will grow,
   as wise men have said.
So ask all your questions,
   and you'll get ahead!

R is for Renge; that's cause and effect.
It means there's no problem that we can't correct.
Find the best cause, come rain or come sun.
You'll get good effects for every good job done.

S is for Shakyamuni,
  a prince long ago—
The historical Buddha,
  as you may well know.
He journeyed and taught
  in his quest for the way,
So all people could be
  enlightened some day.

T is for Teacher,
who helps us to grow
Full of strength,
truth and wisdom—
and some facts we
should know.
Learn life's lessons—
not just reading and math
Someday you'll teach
others to find
the right path.

U is for Unity,
 when we all work as one.
With the same goal in mind,
 we can get so much done!
In some ways we're different,
 in others, the same.
Let's join all together,
 with peace as our aim!

V is for Victory, for winning each day.
"Never give up!" whether it's work or it's play.
Fighting our doubts before they defeat us,
Opening our hearts as each challenge meets us.

W is for Wisdom, which comes from inside,
The power to know and to learn and decide.
We try to grow wisdom, like growing a plant—
The acorn becomes a big oak as we chant.

X is for eXcellent, the best we can be.
If we're eXpecting great things, then that's what we'll see.
EXcitement bursts out and our happiness thrives
When we're eXperts at living eXceptional lives!

Y is for Youth, being young, fresh and free—
Time to learn and work hard, find out who we might be.
Cubs may seem clumsy and weak at the start,
But grown lions are famous for having great heart!

Z is for Zennichimaro, who grew up by the sea.
The wisest of men he knew he could be.
World peace was the mission he, at first, was alone in—
Who did he become? Nichiren Daishonin!

More Fun from Treasure Tower Books!

My First Book of Buddhist Treasures

Gems from Nichiren Daishonin's Writings
Illustrated by Peggy Walker
This book delightfully opens the door to Nichiren Daishonin's writings by presenting 18 fun and practical topics about life and Buddhism. Through brief explanations and colorful illustrations, children can grasp Buddhist principles they will use for the rest of their lives.

$8.95

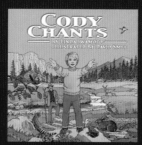

Cody Chants

By Linda Jackson Iwamoto
Illustrated by David Smee
A camping trip with Grandpa turns into a fun lesson about chanting when Cody asks about Nam-myoho-renge-kyo.

$6.95

I Like To Chant

This set of four board books introduces infants and toddlers to the images and concepts of our Buddhist practice through bright and colorful photography. Available separately or as a set in its own slipcase.
(Ages birth to 5)
I Like My Book and Beads
I Like To Chant
I Like the Altar
I Like Meetings

$3.95 each or $13.95 set of four

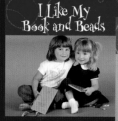

The SGI-USA Kids' Fun Book

Puzzles, games and coloring pages with a fun Buddhist theme will keep your children busy and introduce them to some basic Buddhist philosophy.

$4.95

"Friends for Peace" Fun Book

Your favorite games and puzzles reprinted and updated from "Friends for Peace," the monthly newsletter by and for children inserted in the World Tribune.

$4.95

Order Today: Call 800-626-1313 or e-mail mailorder@sgi-usa.org.